Signs of
Intelligent
Life on the
Internet

Observations, Wit and Wisdom on the Greatest
Communication Medium for the 21st Century

Signs of Intelligent Life on the Internet

Observations, Wit and Wisdom on the Greatest Communication Medium for the 21st Century

by **Alex Kanakaris** CEO, Kanakaris Communications

Dace Publishing/Brentwood Media Group • Ruckersville, Virginia

Copyright ©1999 By Alex Kanakaris
A Dace Publishing/Brentwood Media Group, Inc. Book

All Rights Reserved. No portion of this book may be reproduced —
mechanically, electronically, or by any other means, including
photocopying — without written permission of the publisher.

Library of Congress Cataloging-in-Publication Data.

Signs of Intelligent Life on the Internet by Alex Kanakaris.
ISBN 0-932045-42-1
$7.95

This book is available at a special discount when purchased in bulk for
premiums and sales promotions as well as for fund raising or educational
use. Special editions can also be created to specification.
For details, contact the publisher at the address below.

Manufactured in the United States of America
First Printing, December 1999

Dace Publishing/Brentwood Media Group, Inc.
P.O. Box 91
Ruckersville, VA 22968
888-840-DACE
www.dacepublishing.com

ACKNOWLEDGMENTS

I'd like to thank some wonderful colleagues who helped produce this first volume of *Signs of Intelligent Life on the Internet*. Jeff Hall, Catherine Spicer and Steven Shmerler helped brainstorm many of the concepts that found their way into the book.

Jeff Hall, former vice president with the *Los Angeles Times* and now editor & publisher of the Brentwood Media Group, oversaw the production of the book and contributed his writing and editing expertise. His energy, ideas and vision have been a great source of help to me for this and many other endeavors.

Catherine Spicer is a free-lance marketing strategist and publicist based in Los Angeles. She currently serves on the Advisory Board for the Internet Professionals Network. Her creative ideas, expert writing and editing skills and sense of humor were an immense help to me in presenting and producing this book.

Steven Shmerler is President of SASnet Web Design (*www.sasnet.com*) and also serves on the Advisory Council for the Internet Professionals Network. His wry wit helped capture the spirit of this amazing new phenomenon called the Internet.

John McKay is Kanakaris Communications' Webmaster and art director, and designed the book and its cover. His creative talents have been appreciated throughout all of the Company's projects and Web sites.

I look forward to sharing more with you in Volume II of *Signs of Intelligent Life on the Internet*! For an interactive experience you'll truly enjoy, please visit us on our Web site at *www.KKRS.net*.

Alex Kanakaris
CEO, Kanakaris Communications
The Internet Downloadable Leader

www.KKRS.net

Direct, Over-the-Internet Delivery of
Movies, Music and Books.

To the original founders
of the Internet.

All three million of you.

CONTENTS

e-PROGRESS

(don't stop now!)

They can do psychological profiles online now. I'm very worried. I spent half an hour answering questions, and when I pushed the 'send' button, an 'error' message popped up.

Does it sometimes seem to be like a big game — like it's somehow not real? Do you ever think that you're going to wake up tomorrow to find that there is no Internet — it did not really happen, but you had one hell of a fascinating dream?

Isn't it cool that two companies benefiting highly from the explosion in e-commerce are UPS and Federal Express? In the e-commerce wars, unlike Bosnia, you still need ground troops to support the air war.

A friend of mine who works out of his home office told me he bought a pair of khakis over the Internet, but he rarely wears them because he works in his underwear all day.

I wonder why we think it's so cool that so much knowledge is available at our fingertips. Back in high school and college it was like pulling teeth to get us to go to the library or read a book.

One of these days we may never have to leave our houses, but we will still have to deal with traffic jams in cyberspace.

I hear that someday we'll be able to sit in our cars and simply tell them where to go. I look forward to this, although it does concern me that it will bring a new dimension to the meaning of back seat drivers. Will the person in the vehicle with the loudest voice win out?

They're building a new theme park out in Kansas called the Land of OZ. This is actually a very old idea, but it took off later than expected because of cost. They figured that not enough people would come to Kansas, even with this wonderful new attraction. The Internet changes everything. They're going ahead with the theme park, only now they'll also "beam" the attractions out to viewers everywhere. They predict great success. I'm off to see the Wizard!

Andy Warhol said we'd all get our 15 minutes of fame. Lately it's been more like 15 seconds. Any day now it will be 15 million hits on your home page in a 15-second time span — and that'll be it!

Television in its day was viewed as a modern miracle. Converting from black and white to color was considered a revolution. But the real revolution is what will happen to our computers in the next ten years. Everything up until now has just been the Internet's "black and white" phase.

They used to worry about providing quality content for a 50-channel world. Then they started talking about 500 channels and people broke out in a cold sweat. What about one million web sites? Five million? Can we really feed all these hungry mouths with great content 24/7?

I wonder if the advent of the Internet has had anything to do with the explosion in extreme sports activities. They both seemed to appear at about the same time.

Stop for a moment and try to remember the coolest thing that ever happened to you as a result of an online experience. It was probably something pretty amazing, if you take the time to think about it.

10 things you really need to "get" about the Internet:

1. It's not too late to get started. How many of the original car manufacturers of the 1920s are still around? Does that mean the car business was a bad business to get into? The Internet will always evolve; we're just getting started.

2. To figure out where the Internet is going, stop thinking about where it is today. Be like those who, five years ago, were willing to

make the necessary leap of faith about what it would become. Look where they are today.

3. The technical problems will be solved. In a few years, doing anything on the Internet will be as fast and easy as making a telephone call. This opens a LOT of possibilities.

4. Why bother trying to copy what someone else is already doing? They're already there; they "occupy the space." Look beyond to the next hill to climb and make it your hill.

5. It won't just happen — you have to make it happen. What will it be? How will you do it? When will you begin?

6. It serves no purpose to be jealous of today's Internet stars. Take this wasted energy and channel it properly.

7. Then again, maybe you won't invent something new. Maybe you will be more of a spectator than a player. That's okay, too. The world is already a better place because of the Internet. It's a great show. Enjoy it.

8. There has never been a better time to launch great concepts. It won't get easier later. If you wait too long, someone else will end up producing *your* idea.

9. When you watch Star Wars or Star Trek, it's not the computers that excite you — it's all the other stuff. More amazing progress is just around the corner. We don't know what it is just yet; but whatever it is, it will happen.

10. Don't forget: The Internet is just a tool, no more. It's a means to an end, not the end itself.

5 reasons why the Internet is truly miraculous:

1. In a manner of speaking, it gives everyone on the planet an equal voice. When has this ever been the case?

2. Ideas become more important than things. This is not just revolutionary, it's evolutionary. Mankind will never be the same again.

3. In the end, time is all we have. The Internet saves time.

4. In a world of limited resources, the Internet boosts productivity. There will now be more of everything to go around.

5. Each day, thousands and thousands of human beings experience untold joy as a result of the Internet — joy that was not possible before. Each occurrence might seem small in the grand scheme of things, but taken together, it all adds up.

6 things you will be able to do on the Internet

1. Live teleconferencing with people anywhere, any place, any time.

2. Instantaneous medical diagnoses — and treatment — from any location.

3. Find anybody, anywhere, any time.

4. Instantaneous answers to nearly any question you might have — and by voice, not keyboard.

5. Fill out one basic form that can be used repeatedly and save you from filling out additional similar forms.

6. Vote.

7 things you may not realize that you can already do on the Internet:

1. Order a car with all the color, upholstery and extras you might like and have it delivered to your door in a few days.

2. Dial up a movie and start watching it moments later.

3. Get a total makeover online.

4. Talk live to people over microphones.

5. Listen to a radio station anywhere in the world in real time.

6. Monitor your babysitter and kids in real time.

7. Watch TV.

Remember the debate over calculators when they first took hold? Some thought that school kids had to learn all the formulas because the calculator would make their brains lazy. If anything, freeing the mind of the drudgework has opened new and higher levels of mathematical thought. The Internet will do the same thing for all types of knowledge work. Now, people won't have to spend years and years developing the "right background" or learning the formulas. Knowledge will be more accessible to everyone, regardless of educational background.

With more information readily available to all, will it really make sense for people to spend so many years in school? The person who earns a Ph.D. is nearly 30 years old before he or she begins to contribute to the economy. In the grand scheme of human history, this isn't natural. The Internet should help make smart people much more productive earlier in their lives.

The reality of voice and sight recognition over the Internet is the next big leap. All this typing will soon be outdated. Soon, household members will be able to talk to people live, ask questions, get answers, place orders, make reservations, whatever. They can just talk to the screen on their wall or laptop — just like Captain Kirk used to do on Star Trek. Only maybe we're luckier. There won't be Klingons shooting at us half the time!

Which class back in school was most important? English Literature? History? Algebra? None of the above! Now that I spend all my time on the computer, I wish I had taken "Beginning Typing."

Check out the high school and college reunion businesses online. You no longer have to wonder what ever happened to old so-and-so.

The Internet is a great liberator of thought. What great new idea have you had in the last five years? If you have a hard time answering this question, put down this book for a while, go lock yourself in a closet and don't come out until you've had a good idea. It could more than pay for the price of this book.

Of course, having great technology is not enough. The newest, greatest jet airplane is nothing without a pilot. Pilots are trained, not born. Teachers are the key. The irony is that, with the Internet, we might not need as many teachers. Perhaps one great economics professor will be able to teach thousands of college freshmen around the world, all at once.

One of these days you'll be able to touch your computer screen and, within seconds, doctors will know everything there is to know about your health.

There are so many online shopping malls now. Does anybody really want or need all the stuff they're throwing at us, however low the price? While online shopping gets all the press, the greatest value of the Internet is the quest for knowledge and connectedness.

In the evolution of life, more and more evolves in shorter periods. The impact of the Internet takes this concept to a new dimension.

Y ou can engage in any kind of hobby online. It's so cool. Take bird watching, for example. It used to take years to record sightings of several hundred types of birds. Now you can do it in an afternoon.

Don't you wish you could go back five years and start over, knowing what you know now? The next five years will be even more exciting. Hold onto your seats!

Keeping up with the Internet is like trying to chase a Ferrari down the street. You'll never catch it; you just hope to catch a few cool glimpses along the way.

Trust me when I say that someone, in a garage somewhere, is inventing something that will revolutionize the Internet as we know it.

Remember the first time you printed door-to-door driving instructions off the Net? Was that way cool, or what? Don't lose your enthusiasm for what is happening here.

The setting of standards will be key to making all that the Internet offers universal. Yet the possibilities keep changing. Continued chaos and innovation are a fact of life we must embrace.

The only problem with buying travel packages online is that there are so many choices. It's almost more fun clicking away, thinking about all the places one could go, rather than picking one and actually doing it.

I keep hearing all this talk about "knowledge workers." Thinking *is* hard work, especially since there is increasingly less time to do it.

Today, Franklin D. Roosevelt might have said that the only thing we have to fear is the fear of change itself.

At this moment, there is a child in a room in an inner city of America, which we used to call the ghetto. Around this child is a world of nothing good, going nowhere fast. If I could give my laptop computer to this child and log him onto the Internet, his boundaries would disappear. Instead of four walls, there would be continents and galaxies. There would be online friends of all colors and descriptions.

With the Internet, you *can* teach an old dog (or cat) new tricks.

Thomas Edison said if there is a better way to do something, find it. The Edisons of today will find what they are looking for on the Internet.

Will Bill Gates go down in history as one of the all-time greats? One would think so. Helping to transform the way the entire world communicates and conducts business is probably, in the long run, at least on a parallel with making the first solo flight from the U.S. to Paris.

You see things and you say 'Why?' But I dream things that never were, and I say 'Why not on the Internet?' (with apologies to George Bernard Shaw).

It's amazing that with the growing number of 20-something year-old millionaires popping up in the Internet industry, 30-somethings are already worried about becoming has-beens.

Someday our software tools will migrate into real time so we can find our car keys with an "ALT + F" or fix a dent in our car door with an "Alt + Z," or better yet, use an "Alt + Delete" for a bad date or pesky boss.

2

OLD HABITS CRASH HARD

(ouch)

Ask not what the Internet can do for you. Ask what you can do on the Internet.

Even with all the great search engines out there, it is still hard to find excellent customer service.

If I had to pick the most over-predicted and under-delivered promise, it would be the "paperless office." There's just too much printed about it.

Worried that the Internet could change your career in ways not to your liking? Look at it this way instead — the Internet just created brand new opportunities for you. Forget the old, it wasn't that exciting anyway.

If you're not living on the edge, you're taking up too much disk space.

It is said we use only 10 percent of our brains. We probably use about the same amount of our computer's capabilities, both in terms of software and hardware. If anybody is using even two percent of the Internet's capabilities, that person is probably a genius. If we use another five percent of our brains and another one percent of the Internet, we've just seen a 50 percent improvement in productivity!

I suspect that even after viewing a house in 360 degree 3-D video over the Internet and knowing everything there is to know about the architecture, the local schools, etc., one will still want to step inside the dwelling at least once before signing, via electronic thumbprint, the escrow papers.

The Internet presents an interesting dichotomy. We have more information at our fingertips than ever before. On the other hand, we have never had such potential for the monitoring and invasion of our privacy. But the same people who fear using their credit cards to shop online are those who have been handing their credit cards to teenagers in retails stores for years. Not only that, they have recited their credit card numbers to anonymous people at the other end of (800) numbers to purchase items from television infomercials.

Despite all of the miraculous accomplishments of the Internet, some people still think it sucks. Following are some complaints and my responses:

Virtual life has a tendency to replace real life.
More people than ever are communicating with their friends and family, thanks to e-mail.

No matter how good the technology, it's never quite good enough.
Technology is improving every day. Shut up. Technology is more than adequate for those who bother to learn how to use it.

The promise is always much more wonderful than the reality.
Perhaps the reality is beyond your imagination.

If the Internet creates a caste system of the "haves" and "have nots," much misery will ensue. *Au Contraire.* It actually helps to level the playing field.

We will still stub our toes, burn our fingers on a hot stove. Lovers will still break our hearts. *It's true that the Internet can't stop any of this. At least, not yet. But you will have a better chance of meeting wonderful people from all over the world. And keep your fingers off the stove, you idiot.*

The prospect of "Big Brother" seems so much more real now. *That may be true, yet the Internet also provides far greater individual power and freedom.*

The only thing that sucks is the inability to adapt to change.

In previous generations, some of the more memorable excuses were "My dog ate it," or "My car wouldn't start." Think of the opportunities today: "The dog ate my disk," "My hard drive crashed," "My ISP was down."

3

POLITICS & POWER

(listen up, everyone)

If the financial underclass of our society wants to put the next generation at the head of the table, they must get an Internet connection to their children today, and entrust the keys to a new power generation.

If you are seriously concerned about losing personal privacy over the Internet, I hate to tell you this, but it's too late.

It was suggested in the early 1800s that the U.S. Patent Office be closed because everything that could be invented already had been. With all the inventions soon to come, this branch of government might end up being elevated to cabinet level.

Maybe having all these hate groups online isn't such a bad thing. I suspect it's much easier for authorities to keep tabs on the bad guys these days.

On the Internet everything is virtual, so you can do virtually anything.

Ode to Gen X

We're young and impatient,
Out to conquer the Net.
Millions aren't enough,
Only billions, my pet.

We'll work very hard
For a year, maybe two.
If it takes any longer,
We won't know what to do!

We look and act funny
But don't put us down,
'Cause when we rule the world
You'll still be around.

Now it's back to our PCs,
Just twelve hours to go.
We're coding like crazy,
While we dream of the dough.

Ode to the 50-year-old Guy

Miss the revolution?
Wonder what happened?
While you worked so hard,
Was your mind really nappin'?

Don't despair,
There's gotta be hope.
You could always go back
To good beer and good dope

In the song *License to Kill*, Bob Dylan wrote: *man wants it all and he wants it his way...first step was touching the moon...who is going to take away his license to kill?* A power shift to equality for women and an enlightening of men could combine to change the age-old mindset of region versus region, religion versus religion, and man versus man. The Internet may be the first tool ever created that could help change the very worst of human nature for the better.

The growth of the Internet proves that the power of the written word has actually increased. If you were in the washroom and said something nasty about your boss, all your peers would chuckle along with you. Type the same comments onto a BBS and you could get fired.

Finder's Fee

What if every time we found something cool on the Internet, we could click on a button that contributed a quarter to a good cause? We could wipe out world hunger in a few years.

Some are beginning to think of themselves as cyberslaves who are helping the great pharaohs build their pyramids. Have we learned nothing from history?

It's true that the Internet allows us to get an incredible amount of information at a moment's notice. But what good is information without understanding? And what good is understanding without wisdom? Is what you're planning to do on the Internet going to make for a better world tomorrow?

In 1984, *Time* magazine, in a cover story, chortled about how non-Orwellian our society really was. Think about what's going down these days on the Internet. Maybe he was just a little early.

Talk about a glut of information! The real genius will be the person who can make sense of it all.

Don't forget that during times of revolution, while some are creating new ideas and systems, others are out back building a guillotine.

If all the knowledge in the world is about to be stored digitally, many trees will be spared.

It is said that dictatorships will have a harder time surviving now that the Internet is taking over. If true democracy takes over, how will our institutions — even in America, land of the free — cope?

Though political borders will become increasingly meaningless, tribal instincts of people will actually intensify in the years ahead. Perhaps it is our technological leaders, far more than our political leaders, with whom we will want to align ourselves.

Where is it written that anyone must accept a certain place or stature in life? Nowhere except in a false mental note assumption. The basis of that false assumption begins to dissipate in a cyberworld where the manifestation of wealth and the facade of appearances become less of an issue.

Old-time industrialists today must feel much like the Czars of 1917 in Russia — that the anarchists are taking over!

Notwithstanding the improved physical conditions of men and women, power is increasingly determined by the harnessing of mental strength. Those who use the Internet to quantify their mental strength will be those who have the power in the New Millennium.

I'm hearing more and more about the technology "haves" and "have nots." It's partly an attitude problem. Seems to me anybody with a little desire can find all the access he or she wants. I believe that the real leaders won't wring their hands over this issue, they will find a way to get technology for all people.

Finland is the leader in the wireless world. Finland's Nokia may become the AT&T of the '00s. The Internet has truly opened the borders of commerce to those who are prepared to change the order of our society.

MONEY & CYBERMONEY

(either one is fine with me)

Everyone says the Internet will do away with books, yet, selling books on the Web seems to be one of the biggest things going.
Is anybody else confused?

You can collect stamps, antiques, old military memorabilia, record albums, political buttons — anything at all — online. While a handful will make billions running the online auctions, the rest of us might have been millionaires had we simply not conducted all those garage sales years ago.

The Internet is pretty simple, really. All the normal rules of product design and customer convenience still apply. For the most part, people have simply taken businesses that have existed for years and digitized them. That wasn't hard. It's now that the hard part begins.

Start buying shares in whoever makes that pancake make up all the movie stars wear. Once Internet conferencing becomes more commonplace, that will be the business to be in.

We tend to think of the Internet as a U.S. thing. That's very small-minded. Since there is so much room for growth of the Internet in other countries, that's probably where to look for some great e-business opportunities.

You, too, can be a self-proclaimed Internet guru. After all, who can really challenge you?

By the year 2003, 40% of the US working population will be making their living from an Internet-related business.

I don't know many twenty-somethings who want a "normal job" at a big corporation anymore. Who will run these companies in the years ahead?

Wise men store up knowledge

Smart men buy the rights to it

And sell it on the Internet

Thanks to the Internet, we can work from almost anywhere now. Maybe you should hire your next employee from a little village in India. You might never meet him, but he may beam you some of the best work your company has ever done. Given the time zone differences, he can be working all night, and your local employees can pick it up in the morning.

Newspapers and magazines are predicted to bite the Internet dust one of these days, but have you looked at a newsstand lately? Check out the Internet titles alone! And what about the recent explosion in Internet advertising in printed media, TV, radio and billboards?

Wanna be a media mogul? Start your own radio, TV station or newspaper online, using today's technology. If your content is good, the word will get out. If Matt Drudge can do it, so can you.

If you're confused about market value, maybe this will help. The day Ford bought venerable Volvo for $6 billion, Yahoo bought virtual start-up GeoCities for $4 billion!

One of the great things about the Internet is that it offers hope. Anybody can make a killing regardless of upbringing, degree, whatever. And it's better than the lottery because those who really make it can rightfully be proud of themselves. They've improved the world and have been rewarded for it.

Better to start your own e-business

Than to yearn for money

From the edge

Of your computer.

There is one thing you may want to remember about your customers. Despite the fact that you might have the coolest equipment and the fastest modems, most of your customers may still be using computers they bought three or even five years ago. Don't get too far ahead of them!

The guys who started Yahoo are called "chief yahoos." BIDZ.com, an Internet auction house, is run by a guy who calls himself "Chief Bidizen." The guys who grew up wearing the gray flannel suits in the '50s must think invaders from another planet have taken over.

And maybe they have!

What's in a TLA...

FYI, the IPO is DOA per the CPA.
IMHO the ROI is low & S/N high w/
NCV. BS on the LAN & WC is: the
BOD 86'd the CEO 4 poor QC YTD.
The new BMOC TBA after CV eval,
QA, etc. HR is NA 4 Q&A nor is
CEO, who is apparently MIA in his
BMW, aka DUI. I never liked his
GUI anyway. WYSIWYG.

If you are still trying to figure out the page just prior to this one, I am ROTFLMAO.

A friend of mine told me the other day about something subtle, yet powerful, that's going on. He did an entrepreneurial venture many years ago that was quite successful. For the longest time, when he interviewed for jobs with big corporations, prospective bosses were wary of him. They didn't know if he could be trusted, become "one of them." They were concerned that, deep down, he was still really a closet entrepreneur. Now, my friend reports that headhunters think it's terrific that he has had start-up experience, and they express concern about all the years he spent working at the big corporations!

A man is known by the company he keeps

And the high-tech company he sells.

Every society has its gods. These days, venture capitalists for Internet companies are the new gods of the technical community and the stock market. They decide lives and fates, winners and losers, every day. And punishment for failure is swift.

When it comes to Internet start-ups

Nothing ventured, nothing funded.

Need some quick cash? Print up some business cards and call yourself an Internet consultant. Hang out at those big networking parties and say things like "I prefer the push technology model, myself".... "Don't worry, in two years fatter pipes will take care of everything".... "I'd like to tell you what I do, but you'd have to sign a non-disclosure form first." Soon you'll have assignments up the ying-yang.

As you're planning your new e-business, remember: convenience still sells, now more than ever. Save people time, and they'll reward you for it. Some ideas are still so simple and basic they are profound. Keep it simple!

Just as a man is judged by his clothes,

And a horse by its saddle,

So is an Internet stock

By the amount of
Hype it can hold.

Does it strike anybody else as odd that while some are making bundles, the Internet is quickly moving in the direction of "free?" Sometimes it looks like the Internet could be capitalism's final undoing!

When it comes to e-business, to scratch that itch, you gotta find your niche!

The people I really admire aren't those who have made the millions. It's the people who made the millions, lost them, then made them back again. Now that takes skill.

You know those guys who hoarded all the .com names before anyone else figured out what the hell was going on? Now *there* were some savvy investors who clearly understood the meaning of "buy low, sell high."

If you have made the most of your free opportunities to promote yourself online, right this moment someone you've never heard of might be looking at your resume, getting ready to pick up the phone or, more likely, send you an e-mail that could change your life.

e-options

Today I nearly had a NASDAQ attack,
My e-bay doubled nicely, my Yahoo fell back.
CMGI looked good for a while,
GeoCities sure went out in style.

Wish I hadn't cashed in my AOL options,
Add that to the list of my e-trading sins.
I'm expecting a margin call any day now,
I'll just whip out the plastic and wipe my e-brow.
Every one else I know says they're a winner,
I just hope I can break even by dinner.

There's real money, and there's cyber-money. The bigger the losses, the higher your share price. Isn't life grand?

Ever notice how the Internet generation likes to think it has invented everything for the first time? Take branding for example. Everything today has to be branded. You can't get a job unless you understand branding. What were the guys at Coke, Avis, Quaker Oats and Ford doing all those years?

Do we need to create a special web site for when the next big downturn occurs in the stock market, which it inevitably will? Instead of jumping off buildings like in 1929, people may just delete their personal home pages or something.

Cybermoney may become the universal currency. What will it be backed with, cybergold?

It is part of the national lore that Joseph Kennedy, family patriarch of America's political dynasty, decided to get out of the stock market in 1929 when he heard a shoe-shine boy giving stock tips. Have you listened to the "twenty-somethings" these days? Any parallels?

Probably the best non-virtual job that offers any security is that of a farmer. I think we can predict with some certainty that people will always have to eat. Maybe not forever, but at least for the foreseeable future.

Addicted to day trading? I suppose it beats the hell out of crack cocaine. But the guy who controls your margin count could be just as ferocious as the local dealer man.

Be careful out there.

It does seem like the idea of the stock broker giving advice over the phone to clients is quickly becoming antiquated. What good brokers ought to do is form public companies and sell shares in themselves. Very quickly, the good ones will be weeded out from the bad.

Some of the great pioneers who set up the original electronic bulletin boards paved the way for the Internet, yet many became roadkill once the new technologies took off. Seems like we ought to toss a few shares their way.

The best Internet investments are those that you can believe in.

The geeks who like to put AOL down for not being technologically sophisticated might understand the Internet, but they don't understand people.

18 million people can't all be wrong.

How many times have you had to "rethink your business model?" At some point one must stop thinking and start doing.

5

PEOPLE & SOCIETY

(Yes, they still matter)

Haven't we come full circle, now that we're back to using words and symbols to communicate on the Internet? There's been a lot of talk about the return of the once cherished letter between people, in the form of e-mails. Punctuation as expression has been replaced by a new Internet code.

ALL CAPS MEANS SHOUTING. Emoticons convey "winking," "smiling," and more. People can indicate they are about to rant and rave by warning of an upcoming "flame." All of this is without sound. It's as if we have returned to life before "talkies."

B.C. =
Before
Computer

I Feel So Disconnected.

It all started when my ISP was MIA

And I couldn't get to the www, cause my TCP couldn't remember my IP.

So I called up my ISP and said, "Hey YL/YM, how am I supposed to function if I can't reach my BBS,

Or activate my avatar if I am AFK?

My whole life is on the Internet, IYSWIM."

To which the YL/YM replied,
"Then, IMHO, BFD, you need to GAL.
BFN. And BTW, Yo' Momma."

Geeks love the net. Where else can an overweight, out of shape nerd be a god?

Internet Therapy

I'm so compressed.
My floppy disc
Was just zipped.

Your Chat Room or Mine?

World Wide Weight Gain

Help!

My bot is no longer taut

I need a new back-end system.

Internet Retorts

May a thousand viruses infest your code
And the code within your code.

May a thousand camels
Spit on your SPAM

Your ideas are wide
But your bandwidth is narrow.

Wouldn't it be great if people could use dialog boxes to communicate in person? Maybe a lot of arguments could be avoided if a little paper clip man or walking computer box popped up beside someone to clarify, or offer assistance in describing, what the person *really* meant to say.

Maybe the Internet will help tame ego. For when a person is wrong, many will learn about it quickly. To not take corrective action could invite widespread, damaging consequences. People might learn it's simply more practical to apologize, solve the problem, and move on — the more quickly, the better.

No matter how fast we can click from place-to-place, it will never fully replace face-to-face.

Remember the lyrics of that song: *What the world needs now, is love, sweet love?* Even in the Internet age, this still rings true.

One of the truly great things about the Internet is what it has done for the physically disabled. A wheelchair can't stop a person from cruising the entire world online. Those with eyesight and hearing problems can "see" and "hear." People with frightening diseases can talk to each other, compare notes and form a community.

The Internet is largely a rational device. Ideas, thoughts and messages must be defined before they can be digitized. What impact will this have on mankind, often driven by irrational patterns of behavior? What wins out in the end — logic or emotion?

Young Girl

Get off-a-the-line
Your shopping days
Are draining me blind
So, log off, girl
You spend too much, girl.

I've got gadgets, pagers,
cell phones and more.

I get buzzed all the time,
    such a frightful bore.
I know in advance who's calling
    and why.
Remember when people just called
    to say "hi?"
We talk more than ever, in so many ways,
Sometimes I long for "e-mail free" days.

What makes the hacker tick? It's an interesting question. There are so many positive ways those same talents could be put to use. It must have something to do with their upbringing. So parents, beware: the time you don't spend with your kids could be setting off a time bomb. People still matter.

I think the Internet came along just in the nick of time. I suspect today's aging baby boomers will find it difficult to visit their parents as often as they wish they could. At least now, they can communicate with their parents by e-mail.

G enealogy is another big thing on the Internet. Be sure to check out www.horsethieves.com.

In the coming years, we may see a difference in the people who are pre-Internet and post-Internet. The pre-Internet people may deal more in terms of race, dialect, ethnic heritage, psychological and physical intimidation. I think post-Internet people will deal more in terms of creative, intellectual, social and economic relevance.

Does anybody really believe we are heading for a truly paperless society? Of course not. But instead of mass printing of maps, newspapers, phone books, instruction manuals and catalogs we will print only what we really need. Much waste will be eliminated. This generation might not embrace this, but the next generation certainly will.

The Ten .Com/mandments

1. Thou shalt not take Bill Gates' name in vain.
2. Thou shalt RTFM.
3. Thou shalt always use a descriptive subject line.
4. Thou shalt not send e-mail attachments over 50k.
5. Thou shalt not commit SPAM.

6. Honor thy privacy; always use "BCC" for posting long email lists.

7. Thou shalt not forward jokes without removing the headers.

8. Thou shalt not SHOUT; always use upper and lower case.

9. Thou shalt always proof before committing a Send.

10. Thou shalt not covet thy neighbor's web site.

Revenge of the nerds:

Now, more than ever, the geek shall inherit the earth.

If you're over a certain age and had a fairly over-protective mother, you are probably familiar with the expression: "Be careful — do you want to poke your eye out?" Today's parents are telling their children, "Be careful, do you want burn your eyes out?"

New Math:

Johnny has to mow the lawn every Saturday, which takes two hours using a manual mower with 6" wheels.

If Johnny's dad gets him a new gasoline powered mower with 4" wheels on the same Saturday that his DSL is installed, how long will it take Johnny to mow the lawn?

Answer:

What lawn?

One day the ATM machine appeared and our banking behavior changed forever.

How many other daily behaviors will be changed by the Internet?

As the new generation spends more time online, concerns have been raised about isolation and the effect on our social experience. Viewed in another way, has online anonymity simply encouraged a new form of intimacy?

6

HARDWARE & SOFTWARE

(No getting around 'em)

Have you ever lost an entire hard drive with all your data on it? It's a real pain. Have you considered that maybe it was caused by that geeky little kid you made fun of back in the eighth grade? He still remembers you, too.

As water drips through a
stone

So do inferior operating systems

Wear down your sanity

And destroy your hard drive.

If content is King, then Bandwidth is Queen.

A friend of mine was going to teach a seminar on vaporware once, but he said no one showed up.

It's easy to dodge a spear you can see.

Difficult to dodge a virus

That arrives via e-mail.

A cornered rat will bite a cat.

But a mouse can take you surfing.

With T.V. and the Internet, your computer and stereo system will all seemingly meld into one.
I wonder what that box will look like in three years.

There are too many gadgets now, what with personal digital assistants, beepers, cell phones, voice recorders, laptops, etc. It would be nice if all these things could be combined into one device, but it would be a clunker, wouldn't it? Not for long. Soon all these items will be woven into your clothing.

It will be far easier for entire Third World countries to go directly to PCs with wireless Internet access than it would be to install old-fashioned phone lines and modems.

Becoming a "web traffic cop" might be a good career move. I think we should start issuing tickets to those whose sites don't download fast enough.

Surges and crashes and bugs, oh my!

7

LOVE & SEX ONLINE

(Internet data-ing)

Safe Sex:

I know a woman in Los Angeles who met a guy in New York, online. They chatted up a storm for weeks, and then decided to go on a date. The guy had dinner and wine delivered to both homes and they ate dinner simultaneously while chatting online.

The Internet may change our perspective on finding true love. It used to be that people said there was a person of their dreams, waiting only to be discovered. With the advent of global social connection through the Internet, people will discover that there are actually more possibilities than they ever imagined.

Internet Pickup Lines:

An opening line for conversation in the past was "What's your sign?" Today's opening lines seem to be more along the lines of:

What's your business model?

Is that a pixel in your pocket, or are you just glad to see me?

How big is your hard drive?

Internet Time vs. Real Time

"Five more minutes, honey"
= 1 to 2 hours.

There was a time
When UNIX
Did not have
This much fun.

Personal Ads

Seeking an F partner

Must have a hot baud

No major bandwidth

And great plug-in capabilities.

Can one really find love on the Internet? Sure — why not? Technology may change; people generally don't.

Unwise is he who expects

The babe he met online

To actually be a female.

Just as a man should not
wait until he is thirsty
To dig a well.

A man should
not wait

Until he is lonely
To get free e-mail.

When they really do start having sex online (some people claim already to be experiencing some form of it), will all those little emoticons be considered a form of foreplay?

Breaking Up is Hard to Do

Maybe there ought to be a site called "my-ex.com." It could facilitate finding a new boyfriend or girlfriend for the one you want to dump. Instead of going through all that nasty heartbreak, within minutes your ex-to-be could receive several great offers. You'll both be happier.

Some say trying to find a soulmate online is impossible. Does this say more about what's out there, or the person making the statement?

The new Internet sites like *www.KKRS.net* are like sex. When the content is good, it's very, very good; when it's not so good, it's still good.

8

ARTS &
CRAFTINESS

(aren't we clever?)

The music industry is up in arms about MP3 and being ripped off. Now they finally have something in common with their artists.

Political operative James Carville likes to say politics is "show business for ugly people." I guess that makes the Internet "show biz for geeks."

Isn't it great that we can all be creative geniuses these days? Want to publish a book? Do it! Write, direct and broadcast a music video? Why not? Send your screenplay off in search of a producer? Just hit *Send*!

Opera and the Internet

Torre Eudora

E-mail me some more a

ASCII me next time

Cause my decoding is poor a

Think of all the money we'll be able to save on art in the future. Instead of paying millions for some priceless painting, we can simply digitally "hang" it on the wall. Once we're tired of that painting, we can dial up another.

People are already downloading music from the Internet via one digital master. No more inventory. No more 'out of stock.' No more special orders.

The Beatles were big. They weren't bigger than Jesus (sorry John) but they were bigger than Sinatra. They at least equaled Elvis. The Internet doesn't replace something like the Beatles. It provides a format to extend the legacy to new generations.

The Internet lacks some things. I still can't get a straight answer to the question, "Is Elvis still alive?"

InterNOTS for Newbies

ActiveX: Not the politically involved grandchild of Malcolm.

Archie: Not a white trash character or comic book icon; but just as shallow and linear in thinking as both of them.

BBS: Not the British Television Station, unless you are a redneck.

Bozo Filter: Not a device for screening potential dates, but sort of the same concept in screening unwanted information online. By the way, someone could probably make a lot of money by producing a purse or pocket-sized bozo filter if it did work for dates.

Broadband: Not an online Grrrl Band, but probably will be when a promoter reads this.

Browser: Not to be confused with Bowser, unless you've had a bad experience with Internet dating.

Cookies: Not the typical reference, unless yours actually contain chocolate-covered computer chips that stay behind in your body to reveal your whereabouts to that diabolical baker in your neighborhood.

Digerati: Not a sleek sports car, but go ahead and tell them that it is. They will have a good laugh at your expense and snub you even more.

Flame on/Flame Off: Not the first part of that army marching mantra, although it does sometimes signal a type of online war.

Flash Session: Not a scheduled online peep show. The mainline ISP hosting it is way too boring for that.

FTP: On the Internet, this means sending files, not flowers.

FUD: This is (actually) the acronym for nasty tactics used by computer products manufacturers to cast aspersion on competitor's products, using planted rumors to cause "Fear, Uncertainty and Doubt. " It makes you wonder, after all these years, about the ulterior motives of that seemingly innocent guy, Elmer.

Gopher: Not a rodent, but acts like one.

Hackers: Not those guys who smoke those rolled tobacco things that aren't actually addictive or cancer causing, but people we would like to see die of something.

IP Address: Not a speech that was thoughtlessly cut out of history books because it came *after* the Gettysburg address alphabetically, and they only had room for one. However, if it were, it would certainly be having its revenge now.

Jack-In: Never, never end this term with the wrong preposition, unless you truly intend to make an intimate connection with the other person online.

Java: Not a coffee, but sometimes just as difficult to receive and process.

Server: Not a waiter or waitress, but something we would gladly tip as a bribe to stop crashing.

SPAM: Not a pink lunch meat, but just as disliked.

Teledildonics: Yes, it's exactly what it sounds like, so let's not go there.

WetWare: Not what you're thinking and get your mind out of the gutter. It's hacker slang for your brain, your brain (really!).

Zmodem: Not the French way of saying "the modem."

9

SOMEWHERE
OUT THERE

(let's go exploring)

I wonder: Does the Internet exist on other planets?

I once dreamed that I sent an e-mail to "god.com" asking forgiveness for my sins. I got an e-mail back asking "which ones?" It included a full print-out of everything bad I had ever done, complete with the number of "Hail Marys" I had to say to get rid of them.

Have you visited Silicon Valley lately? The place almost seems to vibrate. A holdover effect from those late sixties days in San Francisco? I believe so, actually. It takes a free spirit to truly change the world. The hippies had it right all along.

If creativity equals intelligence, the Internet makes everyone who touches it smarter. Given the world at our fingertips, our minds can't help but to create.

The only limits on the Internet are the limits of our own vision.

Energy is never lost. So what happens to a Web site when the server goes down?

Timothy Leary tried to arrange for his death to occur while he was online. God bless Dr. Provocateur. Could the Internet be the key to immortality in some way yet unexplored?

What is the sound of one web site caching?

What would our society be like if all the energy ever put into creating 'things' were put toward the metaphysical and paranormal? Would we have learned telepathy instead of inventing the telephone? Perfected astroprojection instead of creating the airplane? Mastered omnipresence instead of creating the Internet?

Interplanetary Net

Ping Me

I want to feel

Less alone

In the Universe

Does an MP3 file stream or make sound if no one is online?

What if someone came up with a single virus that really could wipe out the entire web? Kinda makes Y2K look like a minor blip on the radar screen.

The Internet is the only place where, even if you don't know where you're going, you will probably end up somewhere important.

Despite the technology of large superpowers, Italy remained a world leader in artistic, ergonomic design in the year 2000. Artisans adapted to the age of the Internet in a way that allowed Ferrari's 360 Modena to be both the world's most beautiful production car and one of the world's fastest and most advanced. For example, the manual transmission with a highly sophisticated computer operating in place of a clutch pedal and the coefficient of drag determined by hundreds of hours in a wind tunnel, showed that art and science could co-exist and create greatness. The Internet lesson is that when creative people master Internet technology, we will see the best art and industry ever created.

Where in the www are the gods?

Jesus:
www.Itoldyouso.com

Zeus:
www.greeceyspoon.com

Venus:
www.whoisthisjohngray?.com

Jehovah:
www.knockknock.com

Allah:
www.don'tblamesaddamonme.com

Buddah:
www.Ilost100lbsaskmehow.com

241

Was the Internet inspired by God? If she created the world, surely she is capable of stringing a few wires.

Elvis must be dead.

If he weren't, the biggest
concert on December 31, 1999
would have been his,
and it would have been live
on the Internet.

ABOUT THE AUTHOR

Alex Kanakaris combines a sweeping vision of the evolution of the Internet with an around-the-clock work habit. He has become known for an acerbic wit, outspoken viewpoints, and strong leadership focused on innovation and the development of Kanakaris Communications, Inc. (*www.KKRS.net*).

Mr. Kanakaris provided the visionary leadership which resulted in the first delivery over the Internet of a full-length motion picture in December 1995 at the Kanakaris Web site, in conjunction with XING Technology. Today, Kanakaris offers over 175 full-length movies which can be viewed by anyone in the world connected to the Internet. Kanakaris also innovated in direct, over-the-Internet delivery of books, with the Company offering over 250 electronic titles. NetBooks.com enables readers to resize type, turn pages without scrolling, and search by word or phrase.

As CEO and Chairman of Kanakaris Communications, Inc., Mr. Kanakaris successfully negotiated the acquisition of the

THANK YOU TO...

Thanks to my incredible team whose journey has just begun:
John McKay, Branch Lotspeich ("Legendary Lotspeich"), David R.
Valenti ("DRV"), Naomi Kanakaris, Richard Kanakaris ("the
Brother"), Rose M. Forbes ("the Doll"), Lisa L. Lawrence ("Triple L"),
Liz Olson, Cyndi Copsey, Nikki Stranz, George Atkinson ("Father
of Home Video"), Elliott Weinberg, Gerard Casale ("the Best"),
Tim Waller, Colby Marceau, Bill Crisp, David Shomaker, Arnold
Kahn, Demetri Aryropoulos, Gary Zeidenstein, Corey Ribotsky,
Glenn A. Arbeitman, Bryan Turbow ("Turbo Charger"), Bill Barnett
("Barnyard Dog"), Pepperdine's Alpha Phi Sorority, Michael Lake,
Tony Imbo, Lark Kendall ("Larkee"), Josh Saul, Griff Hopkins,
Dr. Steven A. Newman, James Anthony Golff, Richard Mead,
Caroline Michaels, Van Holster, John Russell ("Big Bad John"),
Frank Firestone Ake, Beryl Wolk, Richard Epstein, and last,
but not least, Sheila Bedworth ("Baby", "L.A. Woman").

No thanks to the negativists, fair weather friends, and people who
could've participated in the growth of Kanakaris Communications
but didn't. Reflect on this: *!sruoy pu*

Alex Kanakaris
December, 1999

25 year old Desience Corporation, a supplier of proprietary computer command installations for NASA, U.S. Navy, FBI, IBM, Apple, Mitsubishi and other government agencies and Fortune 500 companies. In 1999, he signed Internet business agreements with Microsoft, encoding.com, Screaming Media, INXSYS, LMKI Communications, ION Systems, GEO Interactive, and others.

Mr. Kanakaris began writing published articles at an early age with a column called *East European Spectrum* for the world's largest stamp collecting newspaper, *Linn's Stamp News*. Later, he wrote about politics, music and home video. He was editor-in-chief of *Video Swapper*, *Video Entertainment*, *The Video Critic*, *New Talent Streetscene* and *L.A.>POP*. Mr. Kanakaris was involved in marketing for the world's largest costume jewelry company and a large electronics manufacturer. He became a stockbroker for Dean Witter as part of a personal training and experience program in preparation for becoming CEO of a public company.